Hit The Road
INDIA

A Road Rally Through The Heart of India

A Travel Photo-Journal
By Ric Gazarian

Rally Publishing
www.rallypublishing.com
www.hittheroadindia.com

ISBN 978-0-9839289-2-8
1st Edition

Dedicated

To the enthusiastic and effervescent organizers of the Rickshaw Challenge:
Aravind, Princely, Babu, Thyagu (Tiger), J.P, and the indefatigable Sateesh;
To the two hardest working filmmakers: Gor and Moosh Bahgdasaryan;
To my driving partner: Keith King;
And finally to the inscrutable and inspiring backdrop of India.

Table of Contents

Preface

Never stop moving forward, continually sound your horn (typically, for no apparent reason), the law of the jungle rules (the bigger the mode of transportation has the right of way), and finally just hope for the best. It was kismet. These were the rules of the road in India. My partner, Keith King, and I drove 2300 km from Mumbai to Chennai in the Rickshaw Challenge. In a motorized auto-rickshaw.

What is a motorized auto-rickshaw? (It is also commonly referred to as a tuk-tuk in South East Asia.) Imagine an underpowered riding lawn mower without the blade, three wheels, and a semi-enclosed canvas top. It has seven horse power. My kitchen blender has two and a half horse power and I only use it to shave ice cubes for the occasional margarita. The rickshaw has four forward gears, one more for reverse, and a manual windshield wiper. The driver actually twists a knob located inside the rickshaw with their hand to manipulate the sole outside wiper. This harked back to 1903 when Mary Anderson invented the first windshield wiper that was also operated with a lever inside the vehicle.

What were we thinking? Why did we want to participate in the Rickshaw Challenge? Some like to vacation at Disney World, others holiday in the south of France, or maybe some appreciate the sunrise at Petra. We wanted to be tested. The Rickshaw Challenge can be described as a combination of the Dakar Rally, *Midnight Express, Cannonball Run* and *Mad Max*. The Dakar Rally since the Rickshaw Challenge was an endurance trial. Participants drove 8-15 hours today, over mountains, through monsoons, on less than optimal roads. *Midnight Express* since we travelled through a developing nation where anything can happen. At a later point during the race, we would be caught in a vigilant police net. *Cannonball Run* since we competed against multiple teams in a madcap, humor-filled dash across the subcontinent. And finally *Mad Max,* since the roads were singularly crazy and you could die at any time. According to the World Health Organization, India has more road deaths than any other country. I am not surprised after spending two weeks on the road in India.

Incredible India, just like the tagline. And when I say incredible, I mean incredibly glorious and incredibly abdominal. On one hand, you have unique sights, need I say more than the majestic Taj Mahal, unparalleled natural beauty, hospitable people, and fantastic food. And on the other hand, you have grinding poverty, deafening noise pollution, unimaginable traffic, relentless touts, debilitating food sickness, stifling heat, and pounding monsoon rains.

We could not envision a better setting than India to embrace this adventure. It was destined to be an indelible experience.

The Route

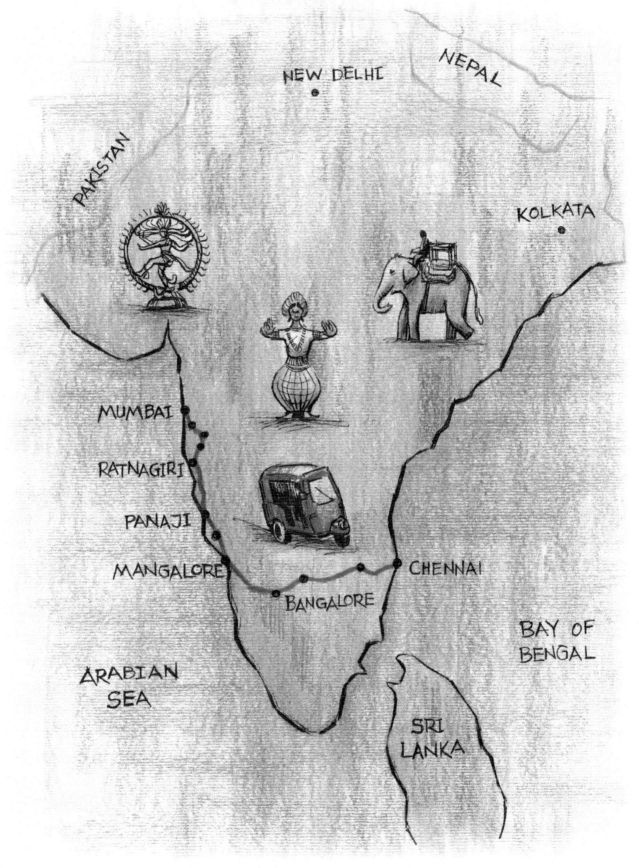

NEW DELHI

NEPAL

PAKISTAN

KOLKATA

MUMBAI

RATNAGIRI

PANAJI

MANGALORE

BANGALORE

CHENNAI

ARABIAN
SEA

BAY OF
BENGAL

SRI
LANKA

Saturday, July 28 & Sunday, July 29 2012

Day Minus 1 & 2

Mumbai

Mumbai's stalker-like humidity would not give us a moment's peace. Restraining orders have been issued for less. This dilapidated megalopolis of faded colonial elegance was the starting point for the Rickshaw Challenge. Twenty-one million residents were squeezed into this former chain of seven islands. Remnants of the former but grand British hegemony remain today, including the India Gate, the Taj Mahal Hotel, and Victoria Station. These sites were subject to Pakistan-based terrorist attacks in November, 2008. An overhang of security precautions remains today, from signing in with a passport to utilize an internet café to shotgun-wielding guards at my favorite bar, Leopold Cafe. Leopold was founded in 1871 and was highlighted often in the bestselling and must read book, *Shantaram,* by Gregory David Roberts.

The participants and rally organizers met at the Sun-n-Sand, Mumbai's first five-star beach hotel. The hotel, celebrating its 60th birthday, had seen better days. It reminded me of a dated Las Vegas Strip hotel that was waiting to be demolished to make way for its modern brethren. An uninviting grey ocean and greyer sky adjoined the hotel. No one frolicked in the ocean.

The thirteen participants and the six organizers crowded into the business center lounge. Six different countries were represented across the six competing teams. The countries included Denmark, Germany, Australia, United Kingdom, Canada, and the United States. Racing gear and road books were distributed. The road book was a customized overview, providing advice and guidance (but no maps), designed specifically for the route. Aravind, the founder of the Rickshaw Challenge, shared some sage words: "If you believe that during this trip something might go wrong, trust me, it already has started going wrong!" The animated and extroverted organizer reminded all the participants that we needed to keep an open mind and our sense of humor as we traveled throughout India during the two week race. Our western sensibilities were to be continually challenged. The Rickshaw Challenge debuted in 2006 and was conceived by Aravind as he slept underneath his Lada Zuguli during a sandstorm on a road trip in Mauritania. The Lada made its debut in the Soviet Union in 1970. It was a common and popular work horse in the Soviet Union and many eastern bloc countries.

After the briefing we were escorted to a dirt area adjacent to the hotel. Six rainbow Skittle-colored rickshaws were arranged in a line. The rickshaw was a compact vehicle. A single seat rested in the front while a small bench was located in the back that could fit two comfortably. They tipped the scales close to 600 pounds. A canvas covered the top while the sides were open to the elements. Our rickshaw was two-toned, an orange top while the body was painted brown. The rickshaw was festooned with logos. The top was covered with official race sponsors. Keith and I were able to customize the body with a series of logos of our choice. Princely, with his classic Indian moustache introduced the participants to the engine and operations of the shaw. Princely, Aravind's college roommate, was the manager of the race and would be accompanying the entire group to the finish line in Chennai.

The participants of all six teams eagerly slid behind the driver's seat, revved the engines, and the proceeded to drive in circles like hamsters in a wheel. My partner Keith was a fish to water with the rickshaw. Keith grew up in Newfoundland, Canada riding ATVs in the wide open woods. In my suburban bell jar, I was not as well versed. Until two years ago, I had never driven a stick-shift vehicle. My one experience was driving for 17 days in the Caucasian Challenge, another rally, in Eastern Europe. Keith, who was taking an anti-biotic, for both food sickness and a cold, retired to the room to rest. I remained to drive in circles, repeatedly starting the rickshaw and shifting into second. Random Indians stared, gawked, and laughed as we made our figure eights. That evening we joined the organizers for a local Indian styled tapas dinner with plenty of icy cold Kingfishers, a popular Indian beer.

The next day, a Sunday found Keith still in bad health. I meandered to the hotel restaurant for a late and leisurely brunch. I joined the Little Miss Rickshaws, a three women team based out of Dubai. Alyssa and Pia hailed from Australia while Ruth was from England. All three were teachers at one of the international schools in Dubai. Princely gathered the racers one more time in the dirt lot for a final bout of training. After driving in the practice area for a bit, the teams departed for some city driving. Keith and I headed to a nearby shopping mall. We planned on purchasing some sporting goods for our future school visits during our trip. The two hour drive was a glimpse of the future. First, the insane driving conditions in the country, and second, our 15 minutes of fame. The locals waved, honked, smiled, shook hands, chased, and supplied multiple double-takes.

As we were cleaning off our shaw, we witnessed Team Five shuffle into the lot on foot. Team Five was comprised of a husband and wife team from Denmark, Soren, a professional soldier, and Eva, a doctor. They were not smiling. They informed us that their parked rickshaw had been stolen outside of a nearby store. Princely and Aravind were alerted and started working the phones. A taciturn Soren and Eva considered their options and wondered what was to happen to their 900 Euro security deposit. It would be an extreme disappointment to exit the race before it even started. An hour later a bouncing Princely reappeared. They had found the rickshaw. It had been towed, allegedly illegally parked. I had spent over a week in Mumbai and had not spied a single tow truck. The unfortunate Danish couple had somehow managed to get their rickshaw towed within 15 minutes of leaving the hotel. Princely and the couple had retraced their steps and returned to the scene of the crime. Spray painted on the asphalt was a telephone number. This was the number of the tow company. After paying a small fine, they retrieved their shaw. That night, Keith and I munched on pizza from Dominos Pizza in our hotel room. A slice of comfort and familiarity.

Ric with the Team Six rickshaw

Princely introducing the rickshaw to the racers

Keith about to go for a spin

The Little Miss Rickshaws in action at a gas station

Racers Eva and Soren from Denmark

Day laborers wait in Mumbai for work

A mother and daughter take a break, sipping chai

Elephanta Caves is a series of sculpted caves depicting Hindu gods carved between the fifth and eighth centuries

The Gateway of India constructed in India to commemorate the visit of British Monarch King George V in 1911

Strolling the streets

A man stops for a quick shave at an outside barbershop

A boy relaxes at a mosque

A sip of water on a humid day

The locals showing off their muscles

Laborers taking a break

Enjoying the day

Monday, July 30, 2012

Day 1

Mumbai to Alibag   110 km

I woke with nervous energy for the inaugural day of the race. I woke Keith who was still struggling with his cold. All six teams had gathered in the lobby for the inaugural briefing with Princely. Keith and I were dressed in matching heavy khaki Rickshaw Challenge shirts, official racing gear provided by the organizers. The participants headed to the lot to make a final inspection of the rickshaws and measure their gas tanks with the dip stick. No fuel indicators were located in the interior of the rickshaw. The shaws took a combination of gas and oil which was added directly to the tank. We were informed that we could expect to manage 25 km per liter of fuel. The tank held roughly eight liters. Our fuel consumption was soon to be an ongoing and frustrating issue for Team Six.

Keith manned the wheel for the flag-off. The six rickshaw engines knocked and banged to life. One after another, the shaws rolled into the wilds of the city. A green and black flag was waved after each team left the hotel.   We might have been the least prepared team.   Prior to the start the other teams huddled around maps and checked GPS coordinates.   We were doing the race without a net – no map – no GPS.

Today, was to be an "easy" day, 110 km to Alibag, our first stop. Each day, the organizers provided waypoints that served as directional beacons. So for instance, we started in Mumbai, our first waypoint was Pen, 81 km away, and then Alibag, and additional 29 km. These waypoints were the only guides to navigate our travels.

Now imagine trying to weave your way through a foreign city that numbers 21 million people, with your only directional point being 81 km away. Our strategy of no map or GPS did not seem sage-like. Very swiftly we realized we had been blindly placed in an urban labyrinth. After many stops asking the locals for assistance, we eventually realized we needed to find Vashi Bridge, one of the four exit points for Mumbai.

Rain started spluttering. The skies grew dark. The race took place during the monsoon season in India. Keith tested the windshield wiper for our inaugural use. Keith twisted a knob with his left hand which moved the sole windshield wiper. The knob was placed inside at the bottom of the front windshield. His right hand remained clamped on the accelerator on the handle bar-like steering wheel.

What originally appeared charming and quaint now seemed maddeningly frustrating: the Indian head wobble. Those in the western world nodded their head vertically to respond affirmatively and shook their head horizontally to respond negatively. It was a binary action. Black or white. The head wobble to a westerner was an ambiguous statement. What did it mean? Yes, no, I don't know? The Indian head wobble looked remarkably similar to a bobble head. Loosen your neck and shoulders, and roll your head, in gentle waves side to side.

After driving aimlessly, looking for signs, we began a strategy of randomly and frequently pulling over and asking for directions. This strategy was limited in its success.

"Namastay! Is Vashi bridge left or right?" I chimed from the backseat of the shaw as my head popped out like a whack-a-mole. I hoped the gentleman spoke English. You had better than a 10% chance that a random Indian spoke English. Over 125 million Indians speak English out of an approximate 1.1 billion population.

The Indian man with the prodigious moustache wobbled his head with a scintillating smile.

"You mean left?"

The head wobbled again.

"So, you are saying right?"

Another smile and another wobble.

Baffled, I jammed my head back into the rickshaw. I yelled at Keith in frustration to push on.

In the blazing, stifling heat, this exercise was repeated numerous times. The heat registered in the 90's with heavy humidity. Eventually, we felt more confident that we had drawn a bead on the chimerical Vashi Bridge and pressed on. The traffic was overwhelming. It was simply mesmerizing. It was a discordant masterpiece of every conceivable mode of transportation miraculously functioning in some sort of apparent concert. Keith attempted to find the right key.

Then, the rickshaw sputtered and coughed. We would become intimately familiar with this sound. It stalled in the middle of the road in dense traffic. Of course, we were in the far right lane (Indians drive on the left). I adroitly slipped out of the back and pushed the rickshaw across several lanes, silently praying I would not be killed on the first day by the trailing traffic. Though the irony would be delicious.

We navigated the road successfully, and the rickshaw rested in the shoulder. We immediately stuck the dip stick into the fuel tank. Bone dry. Keith and I nimbly calculated the math. We had driven approximately 75 km lost in this urban nightmare. If we were getting 25 km to the liter and it held 8 liters, what went wrong? We tabled our confusion, and I waved down a taxi, a rickshaw taxi. I hopped inside.

We scooted down the street to a nearby gas station. I explained and gesticulated to the numerous gas station attendants that I needed gas and oil for my stalled rickshaw. My helpful taxi driver intervened. Since the terrorist attacks of 2008, petrol needed to be placed directly into the vehicle, and cannot be placed into jerry cans. Potential bombs. My taxi driver disappeared and returned shortly with a used empty plastic water bottle. The attendants made an exception for this dumb and bizarre gora (white person). The bottle was topped off with petrol.

Upon being driven back to the stalled rickshaw, I noted that Keith was waiting with two sharply dressed policemen. I wondered what was in store for us. They were simply curious and friendly, an event that would be repeated throughout our trip. We departed after posing for pictures and reconfirming the direction of Vashi Bridge.

What according to Google Maps should have been 24 km and 35 minutes ended up being over 4 hours and 80 km. As we crossed the bridge we pulled over onto the shoulder, I felt a sense of accomplishment, embarrassment, and a bit of fear. We still had 2000 km to go.

A fatigued and ailing Keith folded into the backseat. I was now responsible for the next alleged 83 km. Thankfully, the remainder of driving was mostly highways. I quickly realized the top speed of our rickshaw was about 50 km/h per hour (about 31 mp/h). I also registered a new threat to our overall safety. Trucks and buses. These lumbering behemoths could easily crush our diminutive rickshaw. Momentum was critical for these monstrosities. And a truck was just as likely to run you off the road as they were to slow down. Like a lumbering whale next to our minnow-like rickshaw, these lorries and buses sounded off their horns. Horns in India resembled their user. Bikes, a cute chime. Trucks, a fear-inducing bellow.

Close to twilight we arrived at the hotel in Alibag. Alibag was a small coastal town, especially for India, considering it had only 20,000 residents. We were soon to learn that our hotel for the night was a euphemism for a hovel. It appeared to be the preferred hotel for long haul truckers. Their trucks were parked near our rickshaws. Dark stains covered the thin and tattered sheets, drapes, and even the walls. The AC didn't function. And the hot water on the faucet, dripped dry. We also noted a single bed. I scurried down to the front desk and explained although we were good friends we wished to sleep in separate beds. This was to become a continual theme. We were informed that the hotel only had rooms with single beds (which we discovered was not true). A bed roll was promised. Later that evening, as I lay on the thin bed roll on the floor, I imagined rats scurrying from underneath Keith's bed and gnawing at my face.

Despite being the last team to arriver, Keith and I wanted to celebrate with a beer, preferably cold. We ordered two beers from the front desk. The clerk guided us to an empty, dark room with some tables to wait for our drinks. After 15 minutes, we were still lingering in the gloomy room. I found the attendant and asked him for an update. After several minutes of detective work, I deduced that the hotel had no beer. They had sent someone to the town center to purchase the beers. It was an interesting cultural nuance. I noticed quite often that explanations were not readily provided in India. Instead of explaining that the hotel did not have any beer and there would be a 30 minute wait, they assumed that you had no other plans or options. This was partly cultural. Indians wished not to disappoint their guests. As an analytical individual, I wanted all known information, so I could weigh my options, and make a rational decision. I was to be continually frustrated. The beer eventually arrived; Keith and I recollected the first day with a Kingfisher.

Aravind, the organizer, of the Rickshaw Challenge shares his final thoughts

Keith operating the manual windshield wiper

Our first of many interactions with the police

An exercise that would be repeated over and over

Tuesday, July 31, 2012

Day 2

Alibag to Pune   145 km

Morning came too soon. My face was thankfully intact; no rats had crept from under Keith's bed. I was still tired, a bit achy, and Keith was still ill. All the teams met outside of the hotel for our morning report with an upbeat Princely wearing his omnipresent smile and fanny pack. The teams headed to the lot to prep their rickshaws. We were the last team to depart. Tiger, one of our traveling mechanics, waved the green and black checkered flag as I beeped our horn farewell. I was to be behind the wheel for the day.

As I mentioned, the Rickshaw Challenge was part endurance challenge. This was not your traditional vacation accompanied by drinking frozen mudslides by the pool. We arrived in Alibag near six in the evening and we were gone the following morning by eight. So there was precious little I could share with you about this beachside hamlet.

Our first waypoint was doubling back to Pen, 30 km away. We pulled into the town and the monsoon rains started, a heavy deluge, our windbreakers were donned. The roads were a combination of ripped up pavement, dirt, and potholes overflowing with rainwater. I purchased a stack of fresh bananas from a street-side vendor. Keith purchased some orange and yellow flowers to decorate the front of our shaw. We pulled out of town and headed to Pune.

The rain steadily increased and we wound our way across the hilly roads with verdant backdrop. The Rickshaw Challenge was a race but not in the traditional sense such as the Indy 500. Speed was not the ultimate goal, but who could score the most points. During the morning briefing, Princely shared with us the daily challenges. Today's challenges included photos of funny signs with our rickshaw and also a photo of a temple. We stopped several times in the rain to take photos which were at best moderately funny or amusing … Ball's Farm, a horn, a speed bump, and a children playing sign.

In the continual heavy rain, we pulled over near a random, road side temple to check our bearings. We had to find Chintamani Temple for our final challenge of the day. As I came to a stop in the deluge, a throng of 20 people rushed our rickshaw. In vain, some attempted to join Keith in the back. The rickshaw was a common form of transportation, but 99% of the time they served as a taxi. This enthusiastic mob was hoping to hitch a ride. Smiling, we shook them off, except invited one man who spoke a splattering of English to join us. He was heading in our direction and could also direct us to the temple for the remaining photo challenge.

We eventually followed a narrow, long street packed to the brim with pedestrians, cows, bikes, rickshaws, and cars. What would have made a quaint pedestrian mall back home became a giant

16

game of bombardment. I attempted to avoid all incoming traffic. I rode the brake, alternated with the horn, and tried not to stall the rickshaw in this thick but typical Indian traffic.

At this black and underwhelming temple were several of the other teams, finishing up the photo challenge. Chintamani Temple was dedicated to the Lord Ganesha. It was said if you prayed to Ganesha at this temple you would rid yourself of all your worries. I mumbled a quick prayer to the Lord Ganesha hoping to diminish any future obstacles. With the rain increasing, we positioned the rickshaw next to the temple. Keith in his yellow slicker slid like a seal onto the thin canvas top, hoping not to fall through, and planked for the photo. We hoped we would get bonus points for originality.

We left and started to climb the mountains. The rickshaw chugged, I slid it into second gear. It was barely breaking 20 km/h. Trucks careened wildly by us in the switchback hills. Rain steadily droned on, and the mist butterfly-kissed the tops of the mountains. My tired windbreaker was a poor defense for the monsoon rains. I was entirely soaked. The sides of the rickshaw were open. It was a great feature on a warm day with a cool wind. On a rainy day it was the equivalent of resting in the deep end of the pool.

Successfully navigating the hills, we ended up in Maganlal in the afternoon. Every second shop mentioned Chikki in their store sign. We decided to stop, investigate this mysterious Chikki, and grab lunch. We slopped down some masala dosas and masala tea, attempting to scare the damp chill out of us. A Chikki store was attached to the restaurant. I exited the store with a heavy lump of fresh vanilla and chocolate fudge. Maganlal's claim to fame was its fudge known as Chikki. Their reputation was well-deserved. Fortified with our lunch and some sweet fudge, I revved up the rickshaw.

We arrived in Pune at dusk and realized we would need to heed the dark during our trip. The danger quotient increased significantly at night on the Indian roads. Our single headlight served more as a reflector than a light source. And Indian truckers enjoyed leaving on their high beams in their never-ending attempt to blind us.

Pune, the second largest city in the state of Maharashtra is considered the cultural capital. Its city has been inhabited for over 1600 years, just a teenager compared to the ancient cities of Delhi and Varanasi. We checked into a smart boutique-like hotel. There seemed to be a conspiracy launched by the hotels of India. For the second night in a row, they insisted Keith and I share a single bed. And of course, only one key for the room. Did they want us to be tethered together? This hotel was significantly better than the Alibag hotel, it at least offered internet. Whoops, they offered it, but it didn't work. The front desk after some debate provided me with a refund.

We also managed to be the last team for the second day in a row. We didn't care. We were relieved to be off the road.

A local poses with the rickshaw

Keith earning points for the photo challenge

The mist covered hills

The ubiquitous Chikki stores

Wednesday, August 1, 2012

DAY 3

Pune to Mahabaleshwar 118 km

We woke for the morning briefing with special guests from Round Table India. RTI was comprised of Indians throughout the country that supported projects through volunteerism and financial aid with a special emphasis on education. These regional groups have been giving back since 1957. The Rickshaw Challenge had partnered with this group during our adventure. Throughout the rally we would make multiple RTI school visits.

After the introductions, the six teams, organizers, and representatives from RTI paraded to our first school. We were running 30 minutes late, and the "around 5 minute ride" to the school was closer to 45 minutes. No matter the size of the city or the town, somehow the Indians ensured each location represented dense harrowing urban traffic. Pune was no exception. I pulled into the dirt lot of the school. The rickshaws each performed a semi-circle loop into the lot and lined up in a row.

Based upon the reception we received you would have imagined that we were a high ranking diplomatic party from the United Nations. A long line of school girls awaited us. They were dressed formally in their colorful saris and bedazzled in gold jewelry. Each student held a metal plate known as Aarti. On the plates rested a small candle, incense, and flowers. The racers queued, each facing one of the girls. In a touching ceremony, they rotated the plates, and placed a tikka on our foreheads. An adjacent squad of young students in crisp yellow shirts and black shorts marched to a drum in a military-like procession.

As the other participants and I were escorted to observe some classrooms, Keith, feeling even worse, somehow managed to curl up in the cramped back seat of the rickshaw to sleep. His body zagged like an accordion. The back seat was not exactly overflowing with Corinthian leather comfort.

The Spartan classroom was filled with young primary school-aged children. Two children crammed into each worn brown wooden desk. Giant, glowing smiles materialized across their faces upon our entry. I practiced my ultra-limited Hindi. *"Aap kaise hain? Aapka naam kya hai?"* I questioned the children. "How are you? What is your name?" Smiles, the shaking of a small hand. The infectious Indian head wobble. I marveled at this simple and unique gesture and recognized the importance of this expression to their culture. Another ceremony followed. Songs were sung, speeches were made. I didn't understand either in their native tongue.

We left the school close to two hours behind schedule. I trailed Little Miss Rickshaws and Thermo Electron onto the road. Thermo Electron was comprised of a two-man German team, Erik, a Berlin native, and Thomas, who originally hailed from East Germany on the Baltic Sea. Erik and

Thomas were school chums as well as former flat-mates in Paris. Thomas worked in the aerospace industry and had briefly lived and worked in Bangalore. So, it was a bit of a homecoming for him. My assumption was that they were better prepared with the route and I had no reservations riding their coat tails. Following smart, diligent individuals was a proven strategy for me. It worked for me during four years of college, why not in matters of map navigation.

We ventured into the Pune traffic which was extra challenging due to extensive road construction. After an hour of crawling and covering a couple of kilometers, we entered an overpass. The traffic lightened. I heard a cough. The shaw stalled. I unscrewed the back hatch where the mechanicals rested. Nothing but fumes escaped from the gas tank. I left Keith in the back seat to find a gas station by foot.

I doubled back and soon found a gas station. Small world, LMR and TE were filling up their rickshaws at the station. They informed me that we all had been heading in the wrong direction, and that they had reversed directions since we had separated. Frustration settled in as I returned to the rickshaw. My flip flops were sticking in the wet mud as I shuffled on the shoulder. I was hoping not to get hit by the heavy traffic as I baked in the blistering sun. It was past noon and we still had the full 118 km to drive. The only benefit was that I was able to purchase a two liter jerry can that would be utilized frequently during our drive to Chennai.

We proceeded with some uneventful highway driving and then a series of challenging hills which the rickshaw strained to climb. We turned off onto a smaller road and drove through some local villages. I pulled over to confirm our bearing. A small crowd of loitering men gathered around our rickshaw. Curious and nosy, but friendly and intrigued. A group of school children soon joined us as well. Photos of the rickshaws and the locals were taken. I initiated a cheer with the children of India *zindabad!* Long live India!

More mountains lay before u s. Ample rains fell down on us accompanied by a crepuscular gloom. The roads deteriorated. Pot holes and ditches yawned open in front of us. The rain smacked the windshield while I attempted to control the wiper from inside the rickshaw.

Rickshaws do not exactly glide over these roads like a suspension of clouds. I employed three strategies and none were effective. One was driving slowly into these massive divots. Night was coming, and driving at these slower speeds was detrimental to a reasonable arrival time at the hotel. Second, was driving at a fast speed, hoping to skim over the road. One deeper than expected pot hole and the front wheel could sheer off. And the third stratagem, zigzagging, striving to avoid these obstacles. The other X factor was these pot holes were brimming over with brown rain water on these dirt roads. It was near impossible to ascertain the depth of these potholes, 3 or 13 inches?

Employing the third strategy with a little bit of the second, I careened onto the side of the road to avoid what I surmised was a deep pit in my path. The shoulder was not a shoulder but actually a gully filled with water, but visually appeared to be at the same level as the road. The rickshaw came to a sudden rest, contorted partly on the road and partly dipping into the gully. I gunned the engine, but there was no traction. The back wheels rested in water. Keith and I exited the shaw and appraised the situation. It did not look promising.

We shrugged our shoulders and laughed at our predicament. The rickshaw appeared to be structurally intact. We immersed our legs into the ravine. Cold, mountain rain chilled our legs, knee high. We wedged our bodies behind the rickshaw and after a couple of pushes, it rested on terra firma. The rickshaw was undamaged. The only casualty was my missing flip flop which was in Davey Jones' locker at the bottom of the gully. I chalked it up to a minor loss compared to the potential alternatives.

Soaking wet from our quick swim and the heavy rains, I scooted behind the wheel sans one flip flop. I focused on getting to Mahabaleshwar, a hill station of 14,000 people located at an elevation of 1,400 meters. The weather was cool and damp. In the late 18th century, the British developed this as a health resort.

Finally, feeling the worst was behind us, we imagined getting out of our saturated clothes and drinking some warm tea. The rickshaw stalled. We were out of gas once more. The backup jerry can was empty. I swore softly and repeatedly as I smacked the handlebar in frustration. I had retrieved gas twice before, Keith was now up. He grabbed the can, stuck out his thumb, and started walking, clad in his yellow slicker. A little farther down the road, I saw a car slow down and pick him up. I huddled in the back seat of the rickshaw, wrapping my arms around myself, fighting off the cold, weary of the approaching nightfall. While laughing at myself, anger crept in. How could we have run out of gas twice in one day?

Keith arrived 45 minutes later, thankfully not kidnapped. We added the two liters of petrol with the required oil mixture and departed. Keith had confirmed with the good Samaritans who drove him back that we were in striking distance of Mahabaleshwar.

We arrived at the hotel, last again. We shared our stories with the other participants. The monsoon's wetness had infiltrated the hotel rooms. The beds were actually dank. My research in regard to weather was focused on Mumbai and Chennai, the starting and ending points. Both are hot, humid, and uncomfortable. I was not anticipating the cool, chilling weather of this hill station. A scorching hot shower was deserved. After, the bathroom looked like a steam room. I went to bed fully dressed to offset the dampness of the sheets on the pull-out couch. Again, our room only had one bed and no internet. Keith was still fighting his cold. I was concerned he would only get sicker after a night at this hotel.

Our first visit to a local school via Round Table India

Visiting the classrooms

The rickshaws taking a rest before resuming their journey

Erik and Thomas of Thermo Electron team

The children wishing us bon voyage

A dejected Ric walks back to the rickshaw with a jerry can of gas

Some children posing for a photo with Team Six's rickshaw

The kids erupt in a cheer of "*zindabad* India!"

Keith and Ric push the rickshaw out of the gully

Thursday, August 2, 2012

Day 4

Mahabaleshwar to Ratnagiri   198 km

The teams rolled out. We remained in the small town waiting for the gas station to open at 9 am. We were determined that we would not run out of gas today. The rain was pouring down in thick walls. We stamped our feet to fight the cold. We looked on in frustration as the lone gas attendant lollygagged in his office. We still had 15 minutes to go. At 9:10 am, he was still sipping tea. Staring at us in the rain. I approached a man filling his tires with air. He informed me the station was out of gas! We had just wasted nearly thirty minutes at the station. We found another nearby gas station in town. It was closed and wouldn't open until 10 am. Keith and I debated momentarily and decided to proceed with only a couple of liters of gas. A full gas tank was not meant to be after all.

We headed back into the mountains with Keith driving the rickshaw. Rainwater was thunderously cascading down the mountain face. We were impressed and thankful for the good quality of the roads. The roads could have effortlessly been washed away with these heavy rains. We stopped near the apex to observe the stunning, mist covered views.   A group of Indian men stopped in their SUV-like vehicle to admire the panorama. It was comparable to a clown car, over 15 men poured out. As Keith and I stared out into the horizon, three sari-clad women appeared from the brume ascending up the steep rise in the rain, of course in flip flops. One of the women addressed me in Hindi. I did not understand. She twined a colored Rakhi around my wrist. Rahki, known as the sacred thread, celebrates the relationship between brothers, sisters, and cousins. Odd, my parents never told me I had a sibling in India. She smiled and continued her climb.

We started down the long and windy descent. Soon after, we heard the familiar putter of the engine. We were out of gas. Keith promptly slid the clutch into neutral. We planned to coast all the way down the mountain directly to the assumed gas station. That was the plan at least. We coasted 17 km until we came to a standstill. We had successfully glided to the edge of a village at the bottom of the mountain. The substantial rains had transformed into a hot sun. I walked over to a group of smiling rickshaw taxi drivers with the empty jerry can. The gas station was only two km away.

India was not a game of inches. It was a game of millimeters. Keith and I mentally replayed the morning. If we hadn't been insistent that morning in finding a gas station but instead immediately departed for Ratnagiri, we would not have run out of gas in the hills. Most likely, we would have been able to drive directly to the gas station. The time and gas we wasted that morning were probably enough to reach the station that we were currently two km short.

Hungry, we pulled over to the side of the road. A small shack stood there. I grabbed six random bags of chips and two cokes. Lunch for two. The cost was 90 rupees or $1.63. I calculated the cost at a 7-Eleven in the states. Could I even buy a single coke in the US for less than $2? The bag of chips was only nine cents. Could a factory produce the plastic bag back home for nine cents? Were the margins that much higher in the U.S.? Were the costs that much lower in India? Here in India you could have a delicious sit-down meal for two for the price of one Starbucks coffee. In India, a liter of bottled water was 15 rupees (27 cents). When was the last time you pulled into a CVS and walked out with a bottle of Evian for 27 cents? These Indian companies were selling these products at a profit. How was there such a giant disparity in cost? I purchased a SIM card for under $2 when I arrived in India. This gave me access to a local Indian mobile phone company's network. I was amazed that I was only being charged .018 cents for a local call. Again, not only were they realizing a profit, but the telecom company was able to account for these micro-charges.

The chips came in Indianized versions ... Chatpata Masala, Masala Magic, Masala Munch, Chilli Dhamaka now with more Achaari Masti!! Even the U.S. was in on the action with the American Style Cream & Onion. I was unaware this was America's claim to fame in the chip world, but they were quite tasty with a coke or the local Indian version, Thumb's Up. We munched on the chips as we darted back into the hills with a full tank of gas and a full jerry can.

The engine stopped. In the hills. I pushed the rickshaw off the road as Keith steered. We immediately opened the back and checked the gas. Our usual suspect. For once, it was full. Keith made some basic engine checks such as the spark plugs. We were at a loss. We called Princely with a personal SOS. The Rickshaw Challenge organizers traveled with two mechanics, Tiger and Babu. Two young Tamil bachelors from Chennai. Both had million-watt smiles and great attitudes. Tiger, whom I hastily nicknamed on the first day after butchering his actual name, Thyagu, wore a sparse, scruffy goatee. Babu donned the classic, but ubiquitous bushy Indian mustache. It was a pleasure seeing them every morning. Tiger, Babu, and I shared a morning ritual or call out. I would holler "aap kaise hain?" (how are you?) They would respond with smiles, an Indian head wobble, and a "theek hai" (OK.)

It was a game of millimeters. The bespectacled Princely shared with us on the mobile phone that our timing was poor. They were currently repairing another competitor's rickshaw that had also experienced mechanical difficulties. He told us to relax and they would come as soon as possible. We speculated once more, if we had skipped trying to find gas that morning in Mahabaleshwar, we would have not run out of gas in the hills. And most likely, our rickshaw would have broken down sooner. If we had broken down earlier, we would have been the first rickshaw to have received mechanical assistance.

The support van appeared two hours later. Tiger and Babu accompanied by their toothy smiles poured out of the van chaperoned by Princely. Tiger jammed his head in the engine compartment with the rest of us creating a viewing gallery. He promptly deduced the gear box had been shredded. (Good chance my fault.) Like an industrious spider crafting his web, Tiger with Babu's assistance switched out the gear box. In less than 45 minutes we were back on the road.

After five minutes, we realized we were in the same predicament. The engine lost power; we heard the same grinding noise. We pulled over and contacted Princely. Within moments, Tiger and Babu were back to work. The new gear box had already been destroyed. A new one was installed. During his overview, Tiger then realized we needed an entirely new engine. The rain started to hammer down. Thankfully, the support van carried an entire spare engine.

Our one piece of luck was we had broken down in front of a Starbucks in the hills. Well, not a Starbucks, but a shack. A dilapidated shack. The shack was a small store selling biscuits and drinks with a small rice paddy in the back. An elderly husband and wife operated this business. We ordered a round of masala tea to pass the time and to warm up. The rain and higher elevation had chilled us once again.

Tiger and Babu worked assiduously under the rain and in less than an hour had replaced the entire engine. The benefit of the rickshaw was its simplicity. Simple vehicle. Simple engine. When was the last time you pulled into your service station and replaced the entire engine of your BMW while slurping a coffee?

Tiger placed Keith and me in the back seat. This time, he wanted to test drive our baby to make sure all issues had been addressed. With Tiger driving, the rickshaw hummed and sang around the mountain's curves. Tiger was a natural with the rickshaw, better than Keith, and definitely better than me. After nearly an hour, Tiger departed and Keith took over. We were now fighting the clock. Night fall would come close to half past seven. It was now after 5 pm. We still had 100 km to go. Not promising.

Near 8 pm, we pulled into a gas station to top off the tank. The rains came down so densely we could no longer drive the rickshaw safely. We would now have to wait out this additional obstacle. A small store was adjacent to the station. Aside from the chips numerous hours ago, we had not eaten. A large dark pan with oil was frying up something that looked very edible. I greedily consumed several fried potato treats and then ordered several more as I indifferently burned the roof of my mouth.

Eating food in India was similar to the lottery. A Bizarro World-like lottery you didn't want to win. If you played often enough you would get food poisoning. Personally, I love Indian food so it was a double-edged sword. Every commonsensical rule said don't eat at this gas station store. Years ago, I had met an older British man who had been raised in India. He shared with me two pieces of advice while eating in India: don't eat street food and when hungry snack on bananas. I repeatedly broke these rules. Keith and I conversed often of our anxiety of extreme food sickness while driving our rickshaw.

Strategies were shared and debated. Use straws. No, the straws were not safe, because they weren't stored properly and the staff handled them with their hands. Just drink directly from the can. The tops of cans weren't hygienic so don't put your lips directly on the can. Use glasses; just don't let them touch your lips. Actually, don't use glasses at all. Most dishes and glasses were cleaned by hand. And when I say by hand, I meant rubbing the inside of the glass with their thumb and fingers. Oh, and their hands most likely were dirty. For instance, the bathrooms at the Chennai International Airport did not have toilet paper or soap. So if the airport could not manage to have the basics, what were the odds that soap would reside in the middle of nowhere at this gas station. And the water, of course, you couldn't drink it safely, you needed bottled water. They were not washing these cups and utensils with bottled water. All this analyzing, made you want to throw up your hands in frustration.

I ordered more of the tasty, breaded fried food. I hoped for the best. The rain subsided a bit, and we pushed off into the dark.

Trepidation began to sink in. It was pitch dark and there were no street lights in most of India, and definitely not here. Keith drove cautiously as we realized our singular headlight was not functioning. Giant trucks careened by us. Magnificently blinding high beams obstructed our sight, momentarily dazzling us for a few moments with the passing of every vehicle. We held our breath for these several seconds, for when we recovered our vision we hoped there was not a new vehicle directly in our path. Without a headlight, not only were we driving blind, but we were barely visible on the road.

Then the rickshaw stalled. Keith grabbed the starter. The starter was a long silver bar to the left of the steering wheel, parallel to the floor of the rickshaw. You would yank it up to start the engine. It reminded me of past days when I mowed lawns for my summer job. It was straight forward. Ignition on. Gear in neutral. And a little gas. Keith thrusted the starter up and down with visible anger. To no effect. Dejected, wet, and tired we stood in the dark next to our rickshaw. Keith's arms and head leaned against the top of the rickshaw. His fears now readily evident. We still had 40 km and it was past nine in the evening. There could still be several more hours of driving. The additional time on the road was not alluring, but our real concern was being obliterated by a truck or bus weighing multiples of our rickshaw.

The trailing service van spied us, and rolled up behind us. We informed Tiger and Babu that the engine had stopped working. Tiger asked us if we had checked our gas. We responded that we had just filled up 90 minutes ago. An empty tank wasn't realistic. Babu slid the dip stick into the tank. It was empty. We were too exhausted to be flabbergasted. We were beaten. We emptied the two liters from the jerry can into the tank. The engine crackled to life.

Tiger, Babu, and Princely returned to the service van. They closed ranks, and drove on our tail. Their headlights were like angels from the heavens or since we were in India like Lord Bhahma from Mount Meru. Their headlights served two purposes. First, their headlights spotted the road in front of us, and second, illuminated our rickshaw so we would be visible to oncoming traffic.

We finally arrived at the hotel in Ratnagiri. It was past 11 in the evening. We had been on the road for 15 hours. Our longest day. Ratnagiri sat on the ocean. The hotel sprawled on the beach. We dragged our bags to the room. For the first time, the hotel had not given us one bed. In fact, they had given us three beds. I drank a cold beer while Keith picked at the buffet. We collapsed into bed.

Chennai bachelors Babu and Tiger

Lunch

Tiger attempts to fix the engine

The local "Starbucks"

A quick pit stop with new friends

Alfresco urinals

A man returning from the ice store

Some local street food

The chicken store

Jalebi, the tastiest of Indian sweets

Some more local tasty treats

Friday, August 3, 2012

Day 5

Ratnagiri to Panaji   244 km

Two hundred and forty-four kilometers. It was to be the most distance we would cover in a single day. We were drooling in anticipation, for tomorrow, Saturday was to be a day of rest. No driving. We were going to be staying in Panaji, the capital of world renowned Goa. I had visions of sleeping late, lounging at the beach, and catching up on all those other to do items … laundry and internet. I knew this hotel had to have internet. I just knew it. Well, I really hoped.

We pushed off, sluggish. I steered us in the direction of Panaji. Goa was a former Portuguese colony and had a distinct taste compared to other parts of India. It is located on the west coast and famous for its beaches and historic Portuguese churches. Tourists are also attracted to the international party scene.

We hit a stretch of narrow roads on some of the steepest hills we had seen. I squeezed on the single brake pedal and tensed as we traversed around each corner. I wasn't confident that the brake was going to be effective. Keith informed me to jam the gear into first if I felt we were careening out of control.   We would need another engine, but most likely we wouldn't die. That seemed like a fair trade to me.

I loathed using the word uneventful. But apart from the long distance, it was a somewhat monotonous day. What I meant by that word was we hadn't run out of gas, the engine hadn't broken down, and there were no monsoon rains.

Near mid-day, we arrived at a small but lively town. The rickshaw pulled to a stop near an out-of-place store-front. Two men and a boy squatted in the open room building home-made drums. Keith and I jumped out, cameras clicking. A light green mosque lorded over the small town center. I approached a group of men and asked for directions to Panaji. Our options were either left or right. I stood still, pointed left for a moment, and then right for another moment. I then uttered the word Panaji, and then shrugged my shoulders to express a question. I reasoned this should be relatively straight forward. I mentioned the indecipherable head wobble; I would now be introduced to the Indian hand wiggle, their version of pointing. The men started pointing, but it was similar to a slithering S movement of a snake. I stood flustered. I repeated the question several more times, and forcefully pointed with my left and then right arm. Still the response was the Indian wiggle-point, neither pointing left nor right, but miraculously in both directions. I grew more frustrated.

What I have failed to mention, in addition to partaking on this amazing 12 day adventure, was that we decided to film and create a full-length documentary. So for much of the trip, following our rickshaw, was the chase van conveying brothers, Gor and Moosh Bagdhasaryan, the directors of the film. The van was driven by the third member of our team, Sateesh, who hailed from Chennai.

When planning and organizing this film shoot in India, I learned we needed to acquire film permits. I then contacted a film permit expeditor in India and was soon to learn a potentially expensive lesson. The longer I spoke to this film permit expeditor, the more I felt I was entering a Kafkaesque bureaucratic maze.

First, we would all need to submit applications to the Indian Embassy. Then the Ministry of External Affairs would vet our applications and then hopefully grant us permission to shoot in India. If successful, we would then apply for our Journalist Visas. This was where the fun and games began. After that, we would need to acquire two sets of film permits for every city we visited. We were staying in 12 different cities during our journey, but that did not include the myriad, unnamed villages and towns we would pass though every day. We needed to acquire permits from both the police and the District Magistrate of each location. And finally if we were filming a landmark, a special permit and a security deposit was required. My stomach started turning with fear of this approaching maelstrom of bureaucracy. Then I finally popped the big question. How much? The response was approximately $20,000. This seemed reasonable if you were flying in with a 100 person film crew for the Amazing Race, but this was two guys with a camera. I then got queasy. The film permits were going to exceed the entire budget for the film.

I conferred with the director, Gor. We decided that we would proceed filming the documentary without the permits. We debated the downside … bribes, arrest, confiscation of our equipment, or worse the actual footage? My final concern was the film equipment. I was bringing in two bags full of equipment worth over $10,000. Does anyone need 10 portable 1.5 terabyte hard drives? Many countries have restrictions with imports. I arrived at the Chatrapati Shivaji International Airport in Mumbai prior to the race. I collected my bags at the carousel and headed for customs. I stopped still, my breath exited like I was kicked in the gut. Two giant conveyor X-ray machines lay in wait. I slowly pushed my bags toward the machines, and mentally overviewed the stories I could concoct to explain this superfluous amount of equipment. No good ones came to mind. At the last moment, I noticed that some people were simply ambling between the machines without scanning their luggage. The custom officials appeared to be quite lax. I slid my cart forward with feigned confidence. Looking straight ahead, I threaded the needle between the two hulking machines. Five minutes later I was in the thick, pasty Mumbai air. Another breath left me, but out of relief.

So, as the men continued to befuddle me with their Indian hand wiggles, a lone policeman approached me. My assumption was he simply wanted to say hi as many policemen had done before. This time was different.

"You come," he barked. I feigned ignorance, smiled, and took some more photos. He yelled to a nearby group of Indians enquiring if any of them spoke English. A mustachioed man bearing a red tikka on his forehead, translated for us. I was immediately directed to drive to the local police station with the cop. I grabbed a confused Keith, and the three of us drove to the station while Gor, Moosh, and Sateesh trailed in their van.

Keith and I filed into the station and were directed to a back room where two tan-suited officers waited for us. We sat quietly across from them. Heat soaked into the office. And this was where you started to wonder. What happens next? An amusing anecdote you shared later that evening over a beer, or curled up crying in the fetus position in a squalid cell, begging to speak to the US consulate?

In anticipation, I had squirreled away 1000 Rupees (about $20) in my pocket if I needed to slip it into one of the officers' hands. If baksheesh was required for us to exit the station, I was quite willing to bribe some members of this local law enforcement agency.

Passports were shown, visas displayed, fathers' middle names shared, phone numbers were given. The information was copied by hand in triplicate and then photocopied. The police explained they needed to be vigilant when they witnessed people videotaping. "You know David Headley?" the policeman explained further. I swallowed. I knew who David Headley was and he lived in Chicago, just where I happened to reside. David Headley is a Pakistani man who worked for the Pakistani terror group Lashkar-e-Taiba. Headley made multiple scouting trips to Mumbai, videoing and photographing the city. This information was used by the terrorists during their multi-day attack in Mumbai starting on November 26, 2008, where 164 people were murdered.

Masala tea was brought out by their mute servant. It was quite tasty. We explained the Rickshaw Challenge for what seemed like the tenth time. More questions. I was beginning to wish we had those required film permits. We emphasized our relationship with Round Table India and the charity aspect of the rally. I was hoping our altruistic efforts would be recognized. The policemen were indifferent to RTI.

Time plodded at a sluggish pace. The officers lowered their guard, and the Indian smiles materialized. Water boarding no longer seemed imminent. Both were in their mid-30s, married with children. During a break in the questioning, their children's photos were produced. Then emails and phone numbers were exchanged. "Do you have Facebook?" one of them enquired. Mark Zuckerberg would have been proud.

The policeman sitting directly across from Keith produced two cell phones. Keith took a leap of faith.

"Ahh, two phones. One for wife, one for girlfriend?" He prematurely smiled. I held my breath. There was a pause, then an electric smiled erupted and the policeman high-fived Keith. I exhaled. The policeman resembled Borat for a moment.

An instant later, the policeman shared with Keith his boredom in policing this small hamlet. Previously, he worked in Mumbai. Keith doubled down. "You miss the action?" Keith punched his fist into his open palm. The policeman smiled again and high-fived Keith once more.

By this time, multiple thick files had been created with copies of all our documents and statements. We were carted into the captain's office. He sat behind an over-sized desk. Servants and underlings darted in and out of his office. We were seated across from him. One of our interrogators stood at attention to the side of the captain's desk. The captain motioned for him to begin. The officer made his overview in Hindi as the captain lazily thumbed through the report, not making eye contact. The officer's hands remained clasped behind his back. This theatre had a taste of banana republic to it.

We were released! We had been detained at the station for two hours. And of course, we were now behind schedule. I drove like the wind, well more like a slight breeze at 50 km/h. And then we stopped. We were out of gas, again. No worries this time, we had the back up two liter can. The rickshaw gobbled it up. We were next to a primary school. A score of big smiled boys clad in white shirts and khaki shorts waved at us. We beeped the horn and motioned for them to approach our rickshaw for photos. Every time we advanced, they yelled, smiled, and darted away. A teacher translated that the children were scared we were going to kidnap them. We must have looked like giant white sasquatches to them.

We motored on and arrived in Panaji. Like every other city, no matter how big or small, the density of traffic was consistently appalling. I darted around multiple rotaries. We visibly glimpsed the Crown Goa Hotel sign. We salivated for our day off. The hotel was set back, and a steep hill separated us. I gunned the seven HP engine and roared up the hill. Keith and I grinned, happy to be finished. Then the rickshaw stopped mid-way up the hill. We checked the gas, and realized we were empty. I pushed the rickshaw the final 20 meters. The organizers were waiting and watching us in front of the hotel. They grinned and beamed as I pushed us the final distance.

We were the last team for the fifth consecutive day. We had multiple engine challenges and had set a new record for running out of gas in a single week. Pushing the rickshaw the final feet was a fitting end to a long, grinding week.

I was in a near exhausted state from the week. We met the other teams for a gratifying and relaxing dinner at a nearby restaurant, Delhi Dorbar. Paneer tikka masala and naan bread were greedily consumed. The multiple Kingfishers slid down my throat. I slept like a baby. They even gave us two beds.

A scenic break

The local mosque

A local craftsman making a drum

Keith and Ric being detained at the police station

Some shy school children

Graffiti recognizing the attacks on Mumbai on November 26th

Our fearless friend and driver, Sateesh

Sibling filmmakers Gor and Moosh Bagdhasaryan

Day 6

Relax in Panaji

Goa was a Portuguese colony for 451 years, providing a unique flavor to this region with its Catholic roots. Their reign ended in 1961 when India's armed forces successfully invaded Goa known as Operation Vijay. Nearly 70 km of unbroken coastline make this a popular destination for Europeans and Indians during the peak season between November and February.

The Crown Goa billed itself as a 5 star resort, but one brief experience with the staff spoke differently to that fact. The Crown Goa informed their guests that they generously provided free Wi-Fi in the lobby. With our week-long challenge of getting internet access, I was looking forward to catching up via email and Facebook. I rose and went to the lobby armed with my iPad. I asked the staff for the password, and was informed that the Wi-Fi was not presently functioning. As in many hotels in India, Wi-Fi was free, but there was no guarantee it was operational.

"Outsourcing is ruining America!" Politicians from the left and right bellow from their pulpits. My friends in the IT industry fly to India for business. Some of my friends are employed by Indian companies like Wipro and Infosys. Yet, Keith and I could not reconcile our day-to-day experience with the media's and politicians' prism. During the 12 day rally with 11 different hotels, not one hotel was able to offer completely functioning internet. India was sucking IT jobs out of the west, yet I couldn't poke someone on Facebook. We complained ad infinitum.

The hotel clerk then informed me I could access the internet at the business center. For a fee. I inquired why he wanted to charge me a fee for a complimentary service they marketed to their guests. He then whispered conspiratorially that if he provided me with free access then he would have to provide free access to all the guests. I responded that was exactly what the hotel should be doing. My logic train was not finding an audience. "Listen, for the fee, you can use the business center. It is no problem!" he gleefully shared with me.

I have noticed throughout my travels in the developing world: it is always "no problem" when it inconveniences the customer. With a big smile and a nonchalant shrug of their shoulders, they have many ways of telling you. *Bes prabliem. Kay garne. May mee panha. Mayo wantee. Moosh kill naheen. Teedak apa apa. Hartz chica. Mish moosh killa. Hakuna matata. No hay problema.* I have heard them all. No hot water. No problem. The bus that never showed up. No problem. The food that was different from what you ordered. No problem. The trend was as long as it doesn't inconvenience them and they have already collected their money, it wasn't a problem.

41

Wawawawawa. My bed was hard. The shower was only lukewarm. The internet wasn't broad-band. You have heard me list multiple complaints with regard to the hotels during our journey. You must be thinking what a spoiled jerk. It was easy to gain some perspective and appreciate your station in life in India. But even here, you can hastily forget. You become inured, jaded.

The immense poverty was at times overwhelming. Mumbai, where we had started the race, is the film and money capital of India. In the confines of Mumbai is one of the largest slums in Asia, Dharavi. An estimated one million people are crammed into .67 square mile. Proletariats toil for 100 rupees (less than $2) a day in cottage factories recycling plastic or tin. These non-OSHA compliant factories demand long hours in punishing heat. This slum is a breathing, living, ecosystem, where thousands of residents persevere and exist. According to *The Times of India,* the average Indian salary in 2011 was floating around the $1000 a year mark.

What we expected and demanded in the western world might only be dreamed of in India for many. On my visit to Dharavi, I snaked my way though claustrophobic, darkened alleys only shoulder wide. Cubby sized homes lined the alley, stacked two high. You could find 15 people living in a 150 square foot apartment. It was one room. There was no toilet. In fact, the slum averaged only one toilet for every 1,440 people. The alley eventually spilled out into a lot. Trash was spewed out in the open. Children played in the area, kicking a ball. I covered my nose in disgust. A fetid smell. A child squatted and defecated with no signs of concern. I turned my head away.

In other, less crowded areas we traveled, lean-tos abutted the highway. A couple of pieces of wood, covered by a sheet of plastic. A single pan sat on top of a cow dung fire. Dahl was being cooked. Families lived here. Children. Traffic screamed by and trash was piled throughout the area. Animals milled about. In the morning, you passed a water well, pumped via hand, on the sidewalk. A small crowd of men surrounded it, dressed in longyis, a simple wrap tied at the waist. They bathed and brushed their teeth on the sidewalk and spilled out onto the street. No expectation or hope of privacy.

Sometimes when navigating through these extreme areas of poverty, I pondered how I would handle the situation if our roles were reversed. How would I fare if I lived on the street, had no privacy, no access to toilets or showers, and ate at subsistence levels? Was I resilient enough to persevere? I thought I knew. I would attempt to drown myself in a puddle that first night. The West had made me soft.

Less than 10 km away was Old Goa, home to the former colonial capital of Goa. I decided to make a visit while Keith rested at the hotel. In the hot and humid sun, I joined the other tourists, mostly Indian, enjoying the sights. I viewed the Convent & Church of St Francis of Assisi, Se Cathedral, and Basilica of Bom Jesus. The Convent & Church of St Francis of Assisi was no longer active but it was an impressive white washed sixteenth century church. More impressive was the interior. Soaring cathedrals with rich colored frescoes covered the ceilings and walls. Se Cathedral of Santa Catarina was completed in the early seventeenth century and is one of the largest churches in Asia. The Se Cathedral was built to commemorate the victory of the Portuguese over a Muslim army, leading to the capture of the city of Goa in 1510. The final visit was just a short stroll to the Basilica of Bom Jesus. This basilica was another early seventeenth century structure. The basilica contained the body of

St. Francis Xavier, a confidant of St. Ignatius Loyola, with whom he founded the Society of Jesus. St. Xavier died during his travels en route to China in 1552. The remains of St. Xavier can now be found in Basilica of Bom Jesus where it attracts a large following of devotees. His body is displayed in a public viewing every ten years. Book your trip now for 2014!

The racers joined with the Goa Round Table later that afternoon. As I shared earlier, the winner of the rally was determined by a point scoring system. One way teams earned points was by donning costumes. No, it was not Halloween, but you receive some funny reactions when wearing a costume while driving a rickshaw in India. Keith and I channeled our inner Muppet. I dusted off an oldie but goodie Halloween classic, Elmo. Keith transformed into Cookie Monster. These costumes were part of our provisions we had brought from home. We posed for pictures with some of the hotel staff, and then departed. We were to spend the afternoon at one of their local projects, a home for abandoned boys.

A dirt clearing sat in the front of the home. A dozen spirited kids kicked a football around the pitch. The children upon seeing Keith and me quickly congregated around us. They grabbed, tugged, and jumped on us. A scrum formed around us, and then the picture taking began. Names were shared, and quickly forgotten. Handshakes and high fives.

We were escorted into the house by the children into a darkened grand room. The kids were put through their paces, songs and dancing. Entertainment that pulled at your heart strings. After the singing, there was additional running around, pictures, and jumping on Keith and me. The heads of our costumes were dislodged and put on by some of the children. After a rewarding afternoon, we all departed and headed back to the hotel.

We were going to be back on the road again soon enough.

Church of My Lady of Immaculate Conception, Panaji

Elmo and Cookie Monster visit the boys' home

The kids confiscate the costumes

Elmo making more friends

The ubiquitous poverty

Garbage is part of the mix

Local neighborhood kids

Eking out a living

Sunday, August 5, 2012

Day 7

Panaji to Bhatkal   207 km

After rising from our comfortable beds, Keith and I came down to inspect our orange and brown rickshaw. Princely shared with the teams that we would be competing in another photo challenge. We would be earning points by taking pictures of us, the rickshaw, and a beach. Our route would trace the coast of the Arabian Sea.

Our rickshaw was tilted at an angle. Tiger, the mechanic, was hunched in a squat in the process of replacing our brakes. "*Aap kaise hain* (how are you)?" I asked Tiger. Tiger beamed, wobbled his head. "*Theek hai* (ok)," he responded. I then pointed at the rickshaw. "*Moosh kill nahin* (no problem)?" I asked. He smiled, his head swayed from side to side, like a boat bobbing in the water. I assumed he was agreeing with me, but who can tell with the Indian head wobble. I was concerned with our braking ability while driving down the steep hills the previous Friday. My fears were well-founded. Both brakes had been totally grinded and destroyed. We might have not been able to stop on our next big hill.

Rightly or wrongly, Keith and I believed the worst was behind us. We optimistically reasoned that all of the bad things that could have happened had transpired the previous week. We believed only good fortune lay in our future. In fact, in this lighter mood, we dusted off some additional costumes. Keith had a rewarding Jackie Moon wig with a matching headband. Please see the movie Semi-Pro for this great Will Ferrell character. And I was wearing a global favorite, a Spiderman mask. It is difficult to comprehend the enormous Indian smiles you were greeted with when you poked your head from the back of the rickshaw as everyone's most cherished superhero.

Today was the one of the few days we had interactions with another team. Typically, we were the last team to leave. And then invariably, we would run out of petrol. Our shaw also had a top speed 10 km/h less compared to the other rickshaws. These factors limited our interactions with the other teams during the day. As we sped or more accurately plodded down the road we glimpsed Team Four. We somehow managed to creep up. Inside was a couple from Denmark, Laura and David. Their rickshaw was bedazzled with painted green bamboo stalks and fearsome, blood thirsty panda bears. In the global collective, we commonly view panda bears as lovable creatures in the same vein as a cuddly koala bear. But Laura and David were adamant about articulating the violent nature of panda bears. Beyond that, they would not share why they had such a strong disdain for pandas. We drove back and forth, side by side, exchanging a couple of high fives as well as some gifts of candies.

Shortly after, a lone beret-wearing policeman motioned Keith and me over. We stopped. He meandered over, asking for our papers … international license and passport. Invariably the police simply were curious of this odd vehicle motoring down the street. It usually gave us an opportunity to stretch our feet, take a photo and shake hands with representatives of local law enforcement agencies. We were soon sent on our way with a pat on the back.

Oddly enough, some of our most meaningful interactions with Indians took place at gas stations. A place we visited often with or without our rickshaw. There were a couple of reasons that contributed to this fact. First, keeping with the theme of excessive employment, on average it seemed that each individual pump was manned by six employees. I think they were all employees, but not absolutely positive. In some petrol stations, groupies appeared to hover nearby. Second, to the Indians, Keith and I were extremely beautiful models or aliens. Back home what would catch your attention? What would make you look twice, or maybe even stop? A super model? Imagine being at a party where a runway model was also attending. Who does everyone want to speak with or look at? Or if I saw an alien strolling down Michigan Avenue in Chicago, you may assume, I would stop dead in my tracks, stare, and hopefully find my camera. Quite often in India we were treated in a similar manner.

I just described many of our interactions with the natives. Stares, double and triple takes, handshakes, questions, and smiles. Occasionally, these reactions were tedious, but sometimes it was flattering to know what an attractive women experiences. Why were we considered such a novelty? The simple fact was Keith and I were not Indians. That was sufficient to be a spectacle during our travels.

So, inevitably, when we swung into a gas station, a throng would gather around us. They would study us, observe us, help us, and question us. Sometimes we would spend 30 minutes relaxing with our new friends. Often, several attendants would poke their heads into our rickshaw. There was a different definition of personal space in India. We noticed that the attendants were rifling through our bags. Not for devious purposes but guilelessly because they were inquisitive to see what sundries and supplies aliens (we) would be transporting in our UFO (rickshaw).

Today, we spent nearly an hour at the station. One of the attendants donned Keith's Jackie Moon wig to everyone's delight. We befriended some children. They took turns wearing the Spidey mask, and slurping on the suckers we passed out. And for lunch, I wolfed down some samosas at the shop next to the station. I couldn't resist the price. Eight rupees each or about fourteen cents. Shocked, Keith and I witnessed one of the gas station attendants driving our rickshaw. He randomly and unilaterally decided to take our shaw for a spin when we had stepped away. Thankfully, he returned it moments later.

We passed a small fishing village and decided this would be an opportune time to earn some photo challenge points. Keith hooked a sharp right, and dove the rickshaw directly onto the beach. In less than a minute, the wheels were spinning in the sand. The locals intrigued with the two aliens piloting their spaceship assembled around us. With big smiles, several children gathered with me at the rear of the rickshaw to propel it up the slight embankment. Keith continued his planking tradition, quickly crawled onto the roof of the shaw for the photograph with the beach in the panorama.

We sensed we were getting closer to the rally hotel when the fact was confirmed. Tiger stood on the street, waving the green and black checkered flag. Team Six was the first team to arrive! A celebratory yell and handshake commemorated the moment.

We wiggled our way through the lively and congested town to our hotel on the ocean. There was a well-known temple and multitudes of pilgrims proceeded down the street. Adjacent to the temple were palm trees hugging the beach. A collection of colorful long fishing boats were being hauled onto the beach with their daily catch. I circled the statuesque temple, concrete grey in its color. Surrounded on three sides by the Arabian Sea, the Murudeshwara towered over 237 feet. Resting behind this tower was the second largest statue of Lord Shiva. The tallest resides in Nepal. Lord Shiva rested in the lotus position. A large group of pilgrims ushered me over. They encouraged me to take dozens of photos of their children with near like ecstasy. They would twist and yank their small children's heads to properly align them for the photo that they would never hold. This was an exercise that was repeated throughout India.

I reunited with Keith who was entwined with several Indians. A pudgy and short Indian man was hugging and grabbing Keith in a bear hug. This was all I needed. I encouraged Keith's new dark skinned friend to hug and kiss him with greater frequency. The Indian's smile was as wide as a child receiving penda at Diwali. Penda is a popular sweet made from butter, cream, sugar, and spices like nutmeg and cardamom. Diwali is a Hindu celebration also known as the festival of lights. Diwali translates as "row of lamps" which is kept lit at night to welcome the goddess Lakshmi. Keith was finding humor in the situation while simultaneously desiring to extract himself from this physical adulation.

"Smiling Buddha," the Indian nuclear program, ushered in the first nuclear test explosion in 1974. This has been well documented. What was not as well known was the very nefarious neutron bomb the Indians had surreptitiously designed and have successfully implemented throughout India. Neutron bombs have limited explosive energy, but release a large and potent amount of radiation that is deadly to humans. The Indians had somehow managed to devise a creepy version of a neutron bomb that only targeted the female population. It left all structures and males unharmed.

Being a tourist we attempted to insulate ourselves from all sorts of touts and salespeople. "Come see my textile/pashmina/silver/marble/ spice/gem/t-shirt store. I export to Neiman Marcus/Habitat/ Target in Washington DC/Las Vegas/Boston. If you come to my store you will not have to pay taxes/ commissions/retail price/VAT. My brother/cousin/sister-in-law works/studies in California/Texas/New York City." You heard these sales pitches ad nauseam. I was even eventually able to ignore the impromptu requests for street ear cleanings with a used Q-tip. But there was one approach that always shook my equilibrium.

Walking to my hotel on a side street, a small man with a dark moustache approached me. "You want a massage?" "What?" I responded startled. "I give you good massage only 30 rupees (about 50 cents)." I strenuously shook my head no and darted into my hotel. Then I started to wonder. Where did he want to massage me? On the sidewalk? A rickshaw? In my hotel room? Did anyone ever accept his offer? Then I started missing South East Asia. There you were also constantly and tediously bombarded for calls of massage. The difference was the masseuses were model-like girls, well at least most of them.

Some of the towns and village centers we passed were exclusively populated by men. Every street, store, restaurant, and hotel was comprised of Indian males. I concluded this was the result of the creepy neutron bomb that eliminated all females. In one of these town centers, I slurped chai at a fly infested stall.

"Sir, where you from?" the young, weed-thin Indian man adjacent to me asked. We shared some small talk, and then I anticipated hearing about his uncle's store. But before he could pitch me, I asked him a question. "Where are all the women? There seems to be only men in the town." "Oh, sir, they are all at home. India is very conservative. Only men work and come here. Sir, when you are done, do you want to see my cousin's store?"

On another occasion, I felt a shadow. I looked out of the corner of my eye. I spied the same young man trailing me. He had been following me for ten minutes down a crowded pedestrian corridor. I stopped hard and stood still. I felt like I was attempting to lose a KGB tail or a sex predator. He rambled past me, and then also stopped. He fidgeted and stole a glance at me. After a moment, his confidence builds; he approached me. The man pointed at my watch. I swiftly held it up to his face. He studied my cheap digital plastic watch. He smiled, said hello, rubbed my arm and walked off.

As Ronnie would say, "Wo, wo, wo! Stop the clock." A beautiful, sexy alien.

The brakes need to be replaced

Team Four, David and Laura

India's version of the fire extinguisher, buckets of sand

Friendly folks we met on the road

A photo challenge on the beach

A friendly police checkpoint

New friends at the gas station

A happy recipient of a lollypop

On their way home

Lord Shiva resting by the Arabian Sea

Keith's new friends

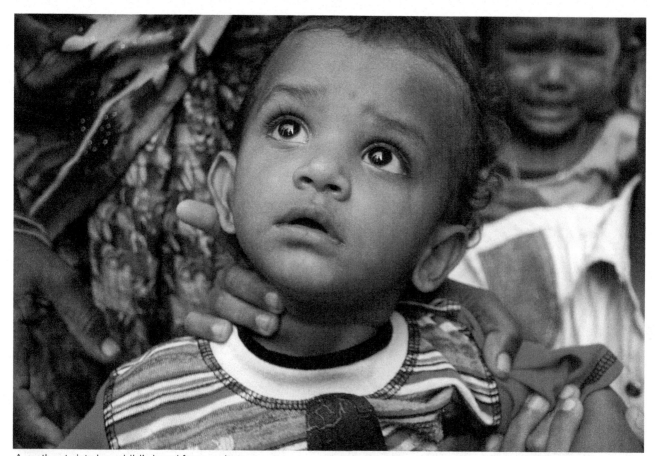

A mother twists her child's head for my photo

Bringing in the daily catch

Young girls out shopping

A local trucker at a gas station

An ear cleaner waits for his next client (see Q-tip tucked in his hat)

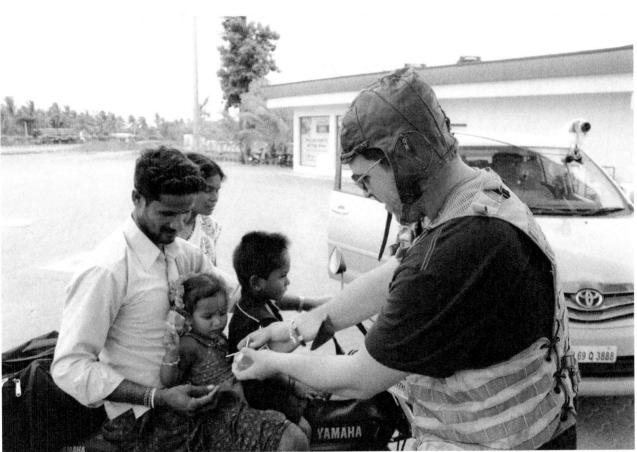

Top & Bottom: Scenes from a gas station

Top & Bottom: Scenes from a gas station

Monday, August 6, 2012

Day 8

Bhatkal to Mangalore 151 km

Like most days, we sluggishly rose around 7 am, or at least that was when the alarm initially chimed on my black Seiko watch. After a couple of false starts, we showered and packed. We also had a habit of missing the complimentary breakfast. We congregated with the other racers and listened to Princely's announcements.

Princely overviewed our challenges for the day. First, take five photos of you, the rickshaw, and extravagant moustaches (preferably attached to a man). Second, discover the name of a temple in the town of Udupi. After spending weeks in India I am convinced that after cricket, the national pastime for Indian men was growing mustaches. It was some sort of innate Indian birthright, similar to the Indian head wobble. It appeared that every Indian male was bedecked with a hearty mustache.

Keith had recognized two new engine issues when driving the previous day. When I took the wheel for the day, I immediately witnessed them first hand. First, our top speed had actually decreased from around 50 km/h to about 43 km/h. Speaking to some of the other teams we learned that they were pushing speeds of 60 km/h. This discrepancy sometimes contributed to our longer driving times. Second, our rickshaw was continually on the verge of stalling. If you grasped the clutch when stopped or decelerating, the shaw would abruptly stall. You constantly had to rev the engine to avert the stall. This attribute become even more challenging and irritating during stop-and-go city traffic.

The second challenge of the day was to discover the name of the temple in Udupi. We maneuvered our way there, and I pulled the shaw to a stop. We determined it was a Hare Krishna temple, named Udupi Sri Krishna Matha. An elephant named Subhadra stood severely chained with its keeper near the entrance. A tikka was placed between her eyes. A slight bell dangled from her neck. The mahout (elephant handler) shouted me over. I found a worn 20 rupee bill crumpled in my pocket which Subhadra adroitly grabbed with her trunk. The mahout then guided my body into a bow and Subhadra's grey trunk returned with a sloppy kiss which was applied to the crown of my head. And who said Indian girls were shy?

A tikka is a red dot of vermilion paste placed on the center of one's forehead. This is where the third, or spiritual, eye is believed to reside. All thoughts and actions are governed by this spot and the placing of the tikka signifies the desire to open the third eye. Most Hindu religious functions begin with the application of the tikka.

We explored the temple and ended up in a large semi-open cavernous room. Hundreds of people sat cross-legged in rows on the floor, orderly and patient. Heavy tubs brimming with food-like gruel were lugged into the room by bare-chested men. The tubs were then pushed down these long aisles. The men slopped out the food to the locals.

Hare Krishna, formally known as International Society for Krishna Consciousness, was founded in 1966 and was based on the traditional Hindu scriptures. Hare Krishna has often been ridiculed in American popular culture. This group has been the subject of investigations for some high profile brain washing incidents in the past. Hare Krishna claims to have over 250,000 devotees around the world with Eastern Europe as its fastest growing region for the movement.

We headed back to our parked rickshaw and corralled some Indian men with outstanding mustaches for photos. As we lounged in the lot, a parade of Indians, young and old, showcased their wares. A bottle of water, a bracelet, a t-shirt. A nation of retailers. It appeared that every second person was selling something on the street. One ambled down the street, since inevitably the side-walks were spillith over with storefronts creeping out like unruly vines. Then additional vendors simply set up shop on the street. Every space was consumed by this ever expanding collective. Then cars, rickshaws, and cows mixed in with pedestrians in this ultimate smorgasbord. It makes superlative people watching for it was completely mesmerizing. But it made everything incredibly difficult, from walking to navigating your shaw down the street. Crossing the street would sometimes require an inner strength. You needed to overcome your fear. One dark, rainy night, I became stranded on the wrong side of the road. It took me literally 30 minutes to wade across with the assistance of a local. Typically, I employed a strategy that I had learned in Vietnam nearly ten years earlier. Vietnam has a unique traffic paradigm. At the time of my visit, over 95% of the vehicles operated were motor-bikes. There were no lanes to speak of in Vietnam, just currents of unruly motorbikes rushing toward you. During my visit I recalled standing paralyzed on the sidewalk in Ho Chi Minh City. I could not determine how to cross this Vietnamese road, the equivalent of 3 lanes in each direction. Hundreds of motorbikes were buzzing like enraged hornets. A foreign couple smiled and recognized my need of assistance. I gratefully accepted their offer of help. The key in Vietnam, as in India was to walk at a steady and unhurried pace and continue until you reach the other side. The oncoming traffic will weave around you. Think of white water river rafting. Your raft does not impact the protruding rocks; your raft slides around the rock, following the current. Neither the Vietnamese nor the Indians stop in traffic, they always push forward, finding the next meter, the next centimeter. The pedestrian was the rock, and the vehicles were the raft.

There are no 7-Elevens in India nor Walmarts. This country was the home of the mom and pop retailer. Every single gas station we went to sold nothing but gas and oil. Not one housed a mini-mart. You could not even buy a water. In fact, Walmart recently lost a lengthy legal battle that would have allowed it access to the Indian market. A giant consumer market of 1.2 billion people. I can empa-thize with India's position. Big bloc retailers would displace millions of Indians from their livelihoods. I was not sure Walmart could hire that many store greeters. *Namaste* Walmart shoppers!

Above and below: Great Indian mustaches!

At the Hare Krishna temple for lunch

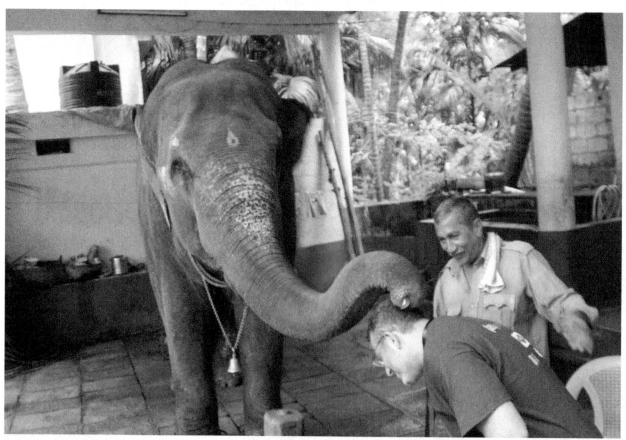

Subhadra planting a kiss on Ric

Tuesday, August 7, 2012

Day 9

Mangalore to Mysore   262 km

The road was torn to shreds. Ripped up. Pot holes that would snap axels. Warp chassis. We were waiting for one of our tires to puncture. It was one of the few things that hadn't happened to us yet. Keith guided the shaw in ambiguous figure eights attempting to avoid the deepest and most dangerous potholes. Monsoon rains began to fall. This obfuscates the threat of the potholes. With the water filling the numerous divots, you were unsure how deep the hole in the road was. You simply didn't know. You just hoped.

Team Six was en route to Mysore. Mysore is a city comprised of one million inhabitants. Its claim to fame includes the first private radio station in India. It was formally known as the Kingdom of Mysore until 1947, when India won its independence from the British.

We started to climb the hills. At lunch time, we stopped at one of the random towns that we passed through every day. Keith and I decided to hunt down lunch. Rain was collapsing in thick sheets of water. Within moments we were entirely soaked. For fifteen minutes we searched for the likeness of a restaurant. My thin windbreaker was hastily defeated. My t-shirt was saturated. My shorts, socks, and sneakers squeaked with wetness. A chill set in and I felt foolish for walking insouciantly in the rain to find this elusive masala dosa.

As I marched down the sidewalk and alternately on the road I made an observation that was a constant throughout my travels in India. First, I had only seen one baby stroller. And it was more accurately described as a bassinet with a hammered on set of wheels. Amazon lists over 20,000 variations of strollers on their website. In the west, it is one of the first purchases that new parents consider. In India, the populace has substituted the carriage with two alternatives. An arm wrapped around their baby or a cloth swathed around the parent encircling the child. Millions of motorbikes plied the roads of India, and often times you would witness a family scooting around town. The smaller children were simply clutched like a small sack of potatoes and the bigger kids were wedged between the mother and father. I also noted that virtually no child wore a helmet.

Second, Indian women were not fond of high heeled shoes. I could count on one hand the number of times I saw women sauntering down the street in the latest pair of Jimmy Choo stilettos. A comfortable pair of sandals won out time after time. The women often complemented their sandals with one of two native Indian variations of apparel. Salwar kammeez was a very common and traditional outfit comprised of loose trousers topped with a tunic and usually complemented by a veil or scarf. Better known was the sari which was a strip of unstitched cloth that was draped over the body in a multiple of styles. A half blouse or shirt was typically worn that exposed the midriff. Both the salwar kammeez and the sari were vibrant in a multiple of hues and patterns.

It was pleasant to visually admire the rainbow of saris and salwar kammeez, yet there was an ongoing mystery. Typically, the younger generation of girls and women donned the more conservative pant suit-like salwar kammeez while the older women dressed in the open midriff sari. Based upon traditional stereotypes in the west, you might have imagined the reverse. I would have expected the younger women flaunting their lithe bodies in the more revealing saris, while the older generation of women would have been more modest in covering their plump stomachs.

The hills increased in steepness. The rickshaw puttered and strained. Two of our competitors easily waltzed by us with their overtly beefier engines. We stopped for gas. We guzzled some hot chai to warm up. I discovered a small clothing shop. To the dismay of the female staff I stripped down in the store and purchased a very dry, baby blue polo shirt. A severe chill had set in and I could feel myself getting sick. I hoped the new shirt would stave off the cold. As Keith drove, I bear hugged myself to fight the cold and rain.

Night had fallen. We entered Mysore. The traffic was thick. Keith darted through the darkened city. We were on a goose chase to find our hotel. We scurried in the labyrinth of the city. We were exhausted and hungry. We needed to rest.

The chewed up roads

The elusive masala dosa! Well worth the wait

Wednesday, August 8, 2012

Day 10

Mysore to Bangalore   149 km

Today, we met with the Mysore Round Table and accompanied them in a visit to a local school. A cavalcade was formed at the hotel, and we drove into the school lot to the delight of the gathered elementary aged school children. After receiving a brief tour, all assembled and waited for the local police chief to arrive to initiate the ceremonies. The usual speeches were made, a couple of songs sung, and then some mingling with the kids. At the end of the visit the shaws scooted into the street and headed toward Bangalore. We were the last to exit. I was behind the wheel. An exuberant throng of kids rushed the rickshaw and jumped in. Close to 10 children had jammed their way into the rickshaw in addition to Keith and me. Ringling Brothers would have been impressed. I revved the engine and beeped the horn to their delight. The children spurred me on to drive the shaw. While I wanted to entertain their wishes, I was quite fearful that one of the kids might pop out and then be crushed when the rickshaw jerked to life. I didn't think that would play too well in the sticks.

After the school visit, we had the opportunity to play tourist. We drove to the Mysore Palace. The palace was the official residence of the Wadiyar dynasty, which ruled the area from 1399 to 1947. Indian independence in 1947 saw their royal position transition into a political role. The Wadiyar's palace was commissioned at the end of the nineteenth century, but was not completed until 1912 under the auspices of British architect Henry Irwin. Nearly three million visitors a year trace the royal footsteps through the grounds and palace. It was a beautiful fusion of Hindu, Muslim, and Gothic styles. Highlights included the Kalyana Mantapa or marriage hall. It was a grand and majestic octagonal shaped pavilion. The hall was graced with a soaring, multi-colored stained glass ceiling with a peacock mosaic wrought in Glasgow.

And since we were playing tourist, we decided to take it one step further. An American tradition (and Canadian, better known as America Junior) the McDonald's drive-thru. As we headed toward Bangalore, we noted a sign for McDonald's and decided to make a pit stop. As delicious as they were, there were only so many samosas one can eat.

For those unaware, there are some regional differences amongst McDonald's menus around the globe. Anyone up for a McAloo Tikka? In Israel you can munch on McFalafelas and McShawarmas. And in Singapore don't neglect to order a McRice. For Hindus, who comprise 85% of the Indian population, the cow is seen as a deity. The cow plays a role in Hinduism as a vehicle to the gods. Lord Shiva rode a cow. On a practical level, the cow provides dung that is used as fuel in lieu of fire-wood. It also supplies milk and ghee (clarified butter). Cows are the king of the castle in India. They can be found lounging in the middle of traffic or being fed treats by passersby as a form of offering. McDonald's, sensitive to local customs, has no beef products on the menu throughout India. No Big Mac, and no Quarter Pounder. You will have to fortify yourself with local favorites like Shahi Chicken McCurry and Paneer Salsa Wrap. Oh, and don't forget the Chicken Maharaja-Mac. The several workers manning the drive-thru window handed us our order, eyes wide open and mouths agape. We were not their conventional customer. We lazily consumed our lunch, lounging in the parking lot, resting on the rickshaw.

If the God creator of *Planet of the Apes* and Sodom & Gomorrah had a three way and spawned a child it would be Bangalore traffic. Someone please burn down this city. It was time for a do over. This IT powerhouse hub was once known as the Pensioner's Paradise. There was nothing paradise-like about it today. The city has rocketed to over twice its size in under twenty years, close to 9 million inhabitants. City planning doesn't seem to be part of the local lexicon. Unfinished concrete over-passes hulked over the city. Octopus sized rotaries were overrun. Sidewalks merged with roads, and roads merged with sidewalks. Pedestrians milled into the road, motorbikes overran the sidewalks, and cows moseyed wherever they pleased. While this was true most everywhere during our trip, Bangalore managed to magnify this chaos.

The final six kilometers of the day took over ninety minutes as night was falling. Harrowing would be a euphemism to describe this journey of dystopian proportions. Every single inch of pavement was fought over. I recalled lesson one: never stop moving forward. Anytime you tapped on the brake, that provided an opportunity, for one, no two, or possibly three motorbikes to dash in front of you. There were no lanes. Well, there were lanes, like most of India, but they were not acknowledged, not even as a suggestion. Two lanes were really six, and three lanes worked out to be nine lanes. There was no margin of safety as every conceivably-sized vehicle inched its way forward. In an area that would safely hold one car back home, in India it would hold a car, a rickshaw, three motorbikes, several pedestrians, a couple of bikes, and a cow. Each vehicle yearned to hopscotch in front of the next regardless of any risk.

The rickshaws we were driving were not going to win any JD Power accolades for safety. There were no airbags, no seat belts, no ABS. It was simply an aluminum shell that would crumple like the flimsiest accordion upon any sort of impact. I cringed to imagine a lumbering lorry crashing into our shaw.

And the noise. Even after being in India for over two weeks, it was formidable to accustom yourself to the noise pollution. It was simply exhausting. The horn was used in a similar fashion to how people breathe. Second nature, unconsciously. Horns were used constantly, continuously and conspicuously.

Back home there seemed to be two types of horns use. One, a brief, courteous tap of the horn as a warning, like *hey you, don't back up I am behind you.* Second, to express anger often in conjunction with extending the middle finger and a heavy handed use of the horn extending maybe ten or twenty seconds.

India had only one version, it was a persistent use of the horn to alert people that they are moving forward and to stand aside. Bikes notified pedestrians. Motorbikes warned bikes. Rickshaws alerted motorbikes. Cars announced to rickshaws. And buses and trucks enlightened cars. Imagine this maddening and deafening chorus of these horns, each with their own signature based upon the size of the vehicle. This deafening cacophony jangled and unsettled your nerves. Your frustration grew for there was often no apparent reason to signal the horn. The never ending horn blowing has resulted in this nation becoming the ultimate boy who cried wolf. Imagine if there was a car directly behind you that leaned on its horn for thirty straight seconds. Would that catch your attention? Would you be alarmed, angry, curious, concerned? Horn blowing was so embedded in the fabric of India that no one bothered to even acknowledge these noises. Of unique note, not once did I witness any motorists sounding their horn in rancor. In fact, we saw several people get hit with no evident emotional response. A motorbike with three men was cutting across a multilane road and was knocked over by a rickshaw (not us). The three men tumbled off. No voices were raised. No insurance papers were exchanged. No apologies were offered. The men simply hopped back on and forded across the road.

My adrenaline increased. I focused. All my senses were elevated. I would navigate this labyrinth. It was dark and we finally arrived. I was drained. The energy left my body. I bent down and literally kissed the cement ground. I promised myself I would never step foot in this city again.

I desperately needed a beer. I spied J.P. in the lobby of our hotel. I grabbed him and escorted him to a restaurant adjacent to the hotel. I ordered two cold beers and began to medicate myself. J.P was part of the team accompanying us to Chennai. J.P. had previously worked as an ex-pat in Saudi Arabia and had now returned back home to India and was working with the Rickshaw Challenge. J.P was in charge of the luggage truck. The rickshaw had no trunk, roof rack, nor much room inside. Every morning we loaded our bags into the back of the truck. They would be waiting for us upon our arrival at the destination city.

As I savored the beers, my thoughts turned to two of my fellow racers. Thomas from Germany and Christian from Denmark. Both had lived and worked in Bangalore. I marveled at their fortitude in living in this unimaginably congested city. Christian and his wife, Irene, teamed together to steer their Ferrari motif rickshaw throughout India. They had met originally in Copenhagen at a Halloween party. They currently reside in San Francisco where Christian works at Google.

Previous page, bottom and current page, above and left:
Scenes from our school visit

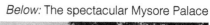
Below: The spectacular Mysore Palace

Fellow tourists at
Mysore Palace

Christian and Irene of
Team Two

A quick stop for lunch

Thursday, August 9, 2012

Day 11

Bangalore to Vellore   162 km

Keith was driving. I thanked Vishnu, Brahma, and Shiva that I was the passenger. I had no desire to associate with the morning traffic in this city. Before we left Bangalore we had another Round Table India visit to a school. Keith and I donned our Muppet costumes once more. Jim Henson would have been proud. The thousands of drivers and pedestrians we passed did not even crack a smile. Everyone in this city was miserable.

The shaws drove into a dirt area adjacent to the school. This was our biggest crowd yet, including a large contingent of the local press. A drum and fife contingent welcomed us. Crisp blue caps with blue sashes matched smartly with their brown uniforms. The local media snapped photos and popped questions. A couple of video cameras rolled. The school kids crowded around us, enjoying the costumes and the brightly trimmed rickshaws. Everyone enjoyed their 15 minutes of fame.

We were welcomed to the school by the local Round Table of Bangalore as the marching band accompanied us into the school grounds. I felt like a king strolling to my coronation ceremony. Successful members of the business community had committed to self-funding this school for over 550 children. The school was founded in 1986, and successfully graduated over 1,000 children. In addition to providing education to these children from the ages of 4 to 14, RTI also assisted in helping the graduates with technical school and job placement. Some graduates even had their children enrolled in the school.

I found myself engaged with one of the RTI hosts, a successful, earnest businessman. He was providing me with his experiences and insights about the school. I was experiencing a slight pang of guilt. Here I was, wearing a fuzzy red one-piece, a stained cut off Elmo head, hadn't shaved in two weeks, and probably smelled a bit ripe. This ill-fated pillar of the community was stuck updating me on his altruistic efforts as if I were Angeline Jolie on a UN mission.

We departed the school and headed toward Vellore, the second to last stop before the finish. We were encouraged by the organizers to stop at Star Biryani, a local tradition since 1890. It was a simple and small restaurant with an open kitchen in the front. I imagined not much had changed over the last 120 plus years. Two men hovered over two large stainless steel vats of rice. Keith and I positioned ourselves at a table; a very attentive and extraneous staff served us. Palm leafs were laid out on the table. A rice and chicken combination was ladled onto the wide leaf. Biryani was a set of rice-based foods with many different ethnic and regional varieties. Its heritage was derived from Persia. Our right hands scooped up the mixture, dipped it into some sauce, and we finally vacuumed it into our mouths. The staff hovered over us. Four staff members stood next to our table and watched us intently as we awkwardly ate with our hands. We were vigilant in not utilizing our left hand. In this part of the world, it was traditional to eat with your right hand (no silverware) and to clean in yourself in the bathroom with your left hand.

Personal space has a different definition in India. What might be considered rude or an invasion of privacy back home was seen as commonplace and helpful. It was slightly awkward to have the entire staff hover over our table and scrutinize all of our actions. Also, a job done by one person in the west might be accomplished by five people in India. I considered the multiple highway tolls we passed on the roads. A man in the tollbooth, a man who raised the bar, and three other men who monitored the first two. I speculated that this over hiring was maybe two fold, one labor was so cheap, and two, hiring extra workers kept the populace engaged.

Was man cheaper than the wheel? An animal? You could envision that you were in the nineteenth century by visually deleting the cars and the cell phones in the street panoramas. Oxen and horses dragged carts. And camels up north. Bicycle rickshaws pedaled cargo and people about. Carts were dragged and heaved by men through the street. And then there was man.

I watched a spindly taut man, maybe 20, maybe 60; haul a giant sack on his head. He was half my weight. I contemplated if I could carry the load. Would I last the day, the morning? What was the productivity benefit of using a wheel, animal, or machine? Were the men paid so poorly it was not beneficial to invest in a cart or oxen?

On another occasion, I stood in line waiting to order an ice cream. There was one person in front of me, and no one behind me. Three feet separated me from the person in front of me. A western definition of personal space. An Indian man approached me, "are you in line?" "Why, yes, I am. Thank you," I grinned. It was the first time I encountered someone in India making an effort to respect lines. He beamed, "this is India!" I returned his smile. Upon my turn, I stuck my head toward the window, and ordered a cone. I immediately felt a body pressed up against my back. I turned around sharply, and the same polite Indian man had now slid up and had smeared his fleshy body against mine. I looked back at him in disgust, "Why are you touching me? There is no one else in line. Just you and me." He smiled again, "This is India!"

"Where you go?" the seventh man asked me in the last five minutes. I was scurrying through the gauntlet of taxi drivers outside of the hotel. I stopped, stared. "I am going to the ATM and then buying a bottle of water. Is that OK?" I responded both dejectedly and sarcastically. "Then what?" he retorted. "Then I will come back to the hotel and read a book," I exhaled. Why? Why was I justifying myself to a complete stranger? Why did he need to know my plans for the evening? This assault on personal space and privacy was nonstop and tedious. But for some reason, I sometimes felt compelled to explain myself.

We finished our meal at Star Biryani while our audience stared intently measuring our actions. It was onto Vellore.

The drum and fife contingent

The local press

A religious procession

A big smile greets us

A group of women outside of a temple

Two boys man the fruit cart

The staff at Star Briyani wish us well

Keith and Ric make new friends

Man cheaper than the wheel?

The wheel at work

Friday, August 10, 2012

Day 12

Vellore to Chennai   132 km

All the participants and organizers gathered in front of the hotel in Vellore. The rickshaws were lined up. Keith and I felt a sense of reprieve. Today was the last day we would be driving our rickshaw. The press, Roundtable India members, assorted VIPs, and some random sketchy hangers-on milled about. I had mixed emotions in regards to our pseudo-celebrity in India. It was a combination of humor and slight astonishment. We had been highlighted in over a dozen newspapers that I was aware of. The mayor of Vellore, P. Karthiyayini, arrived for the kick off ceremony on our last day. She addressed the crowd. Princely called upon me to make a speech on behalf of the racers. Unprepared, I randomly put some words together, remembering to thank as many as people as possible. Too startled to be nervous. The ceremony came to an abrupt finish.

And with that, our shaw, first in line, came to life, I beeped the horn and we pointed toward the highway to Chennai. We passed the gauntlet of photographers and well-wishers. It was our last day. We would soon be in Chennai, the last stop on this long winded sprint across India. A false sense of relief and accomplishment for Keith and me had prematurely set in. India was to share a final kick in the teeth before the day was finished. It appeared we had an uneventful day ahead of us … 132 km across a fair amount of highway. The plan was to rally at a hotel on the outskirts of Chennai and then visit our last Roundtable project. We would hold our closing ceremonies at the school.

For old time's sake, we ran out of gas. We worked out the math. We had a full tank that morning, and we ran out of gas after traveling less than 70 km. The math was less than 8 km per liter. Quite less than 25 km a liter we had estimated. Thankfully, we had the jerry can, and topped off the tank. And fortunately, we had just passed a gas station. After driving in India for a couple of weeks, you quickly adopt the local driving habits. I casually decided to reverse the rickshaw and headed straight into oncoming traffic toward the gas station. By doing so, we would save valuable time, yet our actions defied common sense. But when in Rome …

In the early afternoon, we arrived at the modern and comfortable hotel (too bad we weren't staying here!). We lounged, waited, and reunited with all the teams. As a group, we made the brief drive to the nearby school. The closing formalities were to begin. The racers took their seats outside. The hazy, humid heat encircled us. The speeches began. Little Miss Rickshaws claimed the winner's prize. The three women team rightfully won the award with their well organized and creative efforts. Their prize? Free entry in the Hungary to Afghanistan Rally in 2013. Fear not gentle reader, for Team Six, was also recognized. The 2012 Bonkers Award. This award was a potential euphemism for "we are surprised you finished". With our too numerous to count running out of gas, having our engine entirely replaced, being detained by the police, and our ability to get severely lost, we were the rightful winners of this accolade. Celebrity film producer Ramkumar handed us our award. The grey bearded Ramkumar was the son of a famous Indian actor, Sivaji Ganesan, and was the current head of Sivaji Productions. Each team at the end of the ceremony planted a sapling in the school yard. We breezily milled around. Stress rolled off our shoulders. We spent time congratulating the other teams. Anecdotes from the race were shared. Two thousand and three hundred kilometers had been driven. The last day had even been a bit anti-climatic.

What we had not realized, was we still needed to drive to our hotel. It was 25 km away. Or in other words, two hours of grueling and horrific Chennai traffic. Chennai's traffic rivaled Mumbai and was a younger cousin to Bangalore's ugliness. India had one last surprise for us. We snaked and fought our way through the horn-infested, bumper-banging traffic and finally arrived at our hotel after dark had fallen.

Exhaustion streamed out of us. There was only one thing left. The party.
One rickshaw. Two guys. Twelve days. 2300 KM.
India.
Simply fantastic.

Keith and Ric except the Bonkers Award

Showing off our medals

Round Table India members and film producer Ramkumar

Ric, Gor, Moosh, Keith pose for a final time with their rickshaw

Every day is a surprise!

The Little Miss Rickshaws claim the winner's prize!

Mumbai to Chennai in auto express

SANJEEVI ANANDAN | DC
KRISHNAGIRI, AUG. 9

To Thomas Kuhnelt, 30, an employee of an aerospace company in Munich, Germany, being caught in the Mumbai traffic was "thrilling." What made it even more "fun" for him was that he was driving an autorickshaw in one of the most congested cities in the world, and not merely travelling in one as one would normally expect.

Kuhnelt is no ordinary tourist, a racer like the dozen others from the UK, USA, Germany, Canada, Australia and Switzerland, who have arrived in the country to drive the noisy, hardly roomy, humble auto across its dusty roads and highways in the 'Rickshaw Challenge — Mumbai

Xpress', an adventure rally from Mumbai to Chennai. Divided into six groups, the 13 racers have covered around 1,500 km in six autos from Mumbai via Alibag, Pune, Mahabaleshwar, Ratnagiri, Panaji, Murudeswar (Bhatkal), Mangalore, Mysore and Bengaluru so far. Their journey has now brought them to Mookandapalli on the Chennai-Bengaluru National Highway in Hosur, Krishnagiri district.

"This is not simply an adventure trip, but a learning experience as we are getting to know so much about the tradition and culture of the people of India," said Dr Erik Jentges, 30, of Zurich, Switzerland. Pia Brasher, 31, and Alisha Hughes, 29, of Australia, who share an

Mumbai Xpress participants with their autorickshaw in Hosur.
— DC

autorickshaw with Ruth Brown, 30, of the UK are teachers from Dubai. They hope to make use of the journey to campaign for educating the people of rural India.

Having enjoyed their journey so far, the women are grateful for the friendly reception they have received everywhere.

The racers are also contributing to the fund rais-

The racers have raised $80,000 and hope to make use of the journey to campaign for educating people in rural India >>

ing programme of the Round Table through their trip round the country, having already raised US $80,000 for the club's projects in India through the Rickshaw Challenge. The grateful Round Tablers were there to greet them in Hosur before they set off on the next leg of their journey to Chennai, where they are scheduled to arrive on Friday.

Our 15 minutes of fame

The Author: Ric Gazarian

Ric enjoys travel and the experiences associated with discovering new people and places. His travels have brought him to 75 countries and all 7 continents. He has spent over three and a half years of the last nine years overseas. This included 10 months volunteering in orphanages located in Thailand and Armenia and building a school in Tanzania. He was born in Boston and currently resides in Chicago.

Travel, whether good or bad, contributes to an astounding mosaic of memories. Some of these memories include being shaken down for a bribe by Russian cops on the streets of Moscow, being quarantined by the Chinese government in Tibet for five days, being felled by a case of unbearable food sickness in Yemen, being told by your new friend from Syria that "we hate America" as you drive to Damascus while smuggling cartons of cigarettes, or being advised that the "number one mafia in Taiwan" might want to physically harm you.

Hit The Road: India is his second book, following the publication of 7000 KM To Go (www.7000kmtogo.com). 7000 KM To Go traced his journey from Budapest to Yerevan in a 17 day road rally that covered 7000 km. He is also the Executive Producer of Hit The Road: India, a full length documentary scheduled for release for 2013.

www.hittheroadindia.com

The Editor: James Rosenow

Ms. Rosenow is an attorney and former senior fellow at the Institute for Science, Law and Technology in Chicago where her work focused on genetic and assisted reproductive technology law and policy. She also teaches Health Care Privacy Law at DePaul University College of Law. She earned her JD from Chicago-Kent College of Law. She received a master's degree from Northwestern University's Medill School of Journalism and completed her undergraduate studies at Boston College.

James was raised in DeKalb, Illinois and has been a resident of Chicago for the past 15 years. She serves on the board of Horizon Hospice & Palliative Care. She can often be seen walking with her 150 pound Newfoundland, Chester.

Map Illustrator: Vako Armeno (Khakhamian)

Vako is an Armenian artist born in Lebanon in 1969. He currently resides in Yerevan. He graduated from Toros Roslin Fine Arts Academy (Painting) in 1996, moved to Armenia in 1999 and graduated from the Yerevan State Academy of Fine Arts, 2001 (MFA in Painting/Teaching Art). Between 1991 and 2011, he had 11 solo exhibitions and over 20 group shows in Cyprus, Germany, Lebanon, France, Jordan, Armenia, Greece, Italy, USA and Spain. In 1997, he received the 2nd Prize at the World Youth Exhibition in Paris. In 2010, Vako was commissioned to paint two large murals for the VIP entrance of the newly constructed Opera House in Doha, Qatar.

His paintings are found in: Larnaca National Library, Cyprus; Amman Museum of Fine Arts and City Hall, Jordan; Ministry of Tourism, Beirut, Lebanon; Paleo Faliro Municipality, Athens, Greece; ALMA Museum, Boston, MA as well as several private collections around the World.

www.vakoarmeno.com

Layout and Cover: Karolina "Koko" Faber

Koko is a Polish born, Chicago raised artist, designer, painter and over all multi-tasker, currently residing in Berlin.

www.karolinafaber.com

Photos by:

Ric Gazarian, Keith King, Gor & Moosh Bagdasaryan

CPSIA information can be obtained
at www.ICGtesting.com
Printed in the USA
BVOW07*2254250617

487685BV00002B/6/P

9 780983 928928